I0856587

Colonies in Revolt

Other Books by
Alden R. Carter

NONFICTION

Supercomputers (with Wayne LeBlanc)
Modern China
Modern Electronics (with Wayne LeBlanc)
Radio: From Marconi to the Space Age
Illinois
Darkest Hours
At the Forge of Liberty
Birth of the Republic

FICTION

Growing Season
Wart, Son of Toad
Sheila's Dying

Alden R. Carter

☆ COLONIES IN REVOLT ☆

Franklin Watts
New York/London/Toronto
Sydney/1988
A First Book

Library of Congress Cataloging-in-Publication Data

Carter, Alden R.
Colonies in revolt / Alden R. Carter.
p. cm. — (A First book)
Bibliography: p.
Includes index.
Summary: Examines how the once strong colony-mother-country relationship between America and Britain began to sour through the 1760s and 1770s, planting the roots for the once unthinkable idea of revolution.
ISBN 0-531-10576-8
1. United States—History—Revolution, 1775–1783—Causes—Juvenile literature. 2. United States—Politics and government—Revolution. 1775–1783—Juvenile literature. [1. United States—History—Revolution, 1775–1783—Causes. 2. United States—Politics and government—Revolution, 1775–1783.] I. Title. II. Series.
E210.C37 1988
973.3′11—dc19 88-5624 CIP AC

Printed in the United States of America
6 5 4 3 2 1

For Al Shadis,
who would have attended
the Boston Tea Party.

Cover photograph courtesy of:
The Granger Collection

Maps by Joe LeMonnier

Diagram by Vantage Art, Inc.

Photographs courtesy of:
Prints Division, The New York Public Library,
Astor, Lenox and Tilden Foundations: pp. 12, 50, 58;
Colonial Williamsburg: pp. 17, 66 (top right);
New York Public Library Picture Collection:
pp. 20, 63, 65, 69, 76, 81;
The I.N. Phelps Stokes Collection of American
Historical Prints, Prints Division,
The New York Public Library: p. 26 (top);
Library of Congress: p. 26
(Map Division, bottom), 39 (top);
The Bettmann Archive, Inc.: pp. 39 (bottom),
55, 58, 69, 84; City of Liverpool Museums: p. 40;
The British Museum: p. 45; Independence National
Historical Park: p. 66 (lower left and right);
Lexington Historical Society, Inc.: p. 81.

Contents

Many thanks to all who helped with
Colonies in Revolt, particularly
my editor, Marjory Kline; my mother,
Hilda Carter Fletcher; and my
friends Don Beyer, Dean Markwardt,
Sue Babcock, and Georgette Frazer.
As always, my wife, Carol, deserves
much of the credit.

☆ 1 ☆

Under the Lion's Paw

Many in the crowd on the Boston street were boys not yet in their teens. They shouted, cursed, and pitched rocks and snowballs against the house of the man accused of informing for the hated British customs service. Windows shattered, rocks splintered walls and furniture. Bystanders in the street could hear the wails of frightened women and the violent cursing of an angry man. Then a musket barrel flamed from a window, and the crowd fell back in panic as the sound of a gunshot echoed down the street.

A hush fell. At the window Ebenezer Richardson stood with a smoking gun in his hands. The crowd moved back in, circling a slender form lying still in the snow and slush. On the morning of February 22, 1770, eleven-year-old Christopher Seider had become one of the first victims in a conflict that would grow into the American Revolution.

We do not know why young Seider had joined the crowd. Perhaps it had been a lark, a way to avoid the boredom of the shop or the schoolhouse for an hour or two. Or perhaps he

A MONUMENTAL INSCRIPTION

ON THE

Fifth of March.

Together with a few LINES

On the Enlargement of

EBENEZER RICHARDSON,

Convicted of MURDER.

AMERICANS!
BEAR IN REMEMBRANCE
The HORRID MASSACRE!
Perpetrated in King-ſtreet, BOSTON,
New-England,
On the Evening of March the Fifth, 1770.
When FIVE of your fellow countrymen,
GRAY, MAVERICK, CALDWELL, ATTUCKS,
and CARR,
Lay wallowing in their Gore!
Being *baſely*, and moſt *inhumanly*
MURDERED!
And SIX others badly WOUNDED!
By a Party of the XXIXth Regiment,
Under the command of Capt. Tho. Preſton.
REMEMBER!
That Two of the MURDERERS
Were convicted of MANSLAUGHTER!
By a Jury, of whom I ſhall ſay
NOTHING,
Branded in the hand!
And *diſmiſſed*,
The others were ACQUITTED,
And their Captain PENSIONED!
Alſo,
BEAR IN REMEMBRANCE
That on the 22d Day of February, 1770.
The infamous
EBENEZER RICHARDSON, Informer,
And tool to Miniſterial hirelings,
Moſt *barbarouſly*
MURDERED
CHRISTOPHER SEIDER,
An innocent youth!
Of which crime he was found guilty
By his Country
On Friday April 20th, 1770;
But remained *Unſentenced*
On Saturday the 22d Day of February, 1772.
When the GRAND INQUEST
For Suffolk county,
Were informed, at requeſt,
By the Judges of the Superior Court,
That EBENEZER RICHARDSON's *Caſe*
Then lay before his MAJESTY.
Therefore ſaid *Richardſon*
This day, MARCH FIFTH! 1772,
Remains UNHANGED!!!
Let THESE things be told to Poſterity!
And handed down
From Generation to Generation,
'Till Time ſhall be no more!
Forever may AMERICA be preſerved,
From weak and wicked monarchs,
Tyrannical Miniſters,
Abandoned Governors,
Their Underlings and Hirelings!
And may the
Machinations of artful, *deſigning* wretches,
Who would ENSLAVE THIS People,
Come to an end,
Let their NAMES and MEMORIES
Be buried in eternal oblivion,
And the PRESS,
For a *SCOURGE* to Tyrannical Rulers,
Remain FREE.

AWAKE my drowſy Thoughts! Awake my muſe!
Awake O earth, and tremble at the news!
In grand defiance to the laws of God,
The Guilty, Guilty murd'rer walks abroad.
That city mourns, (the cry comes from the ground,)
Where law and juſtice never can be found:
Oh! ſword of vengeance, fall thou on the race
Of thoſe who hinder juſtice from its place.
O MURD'RER! RICHARDSON! with their lateſt breath
Millions will curſe you when you ſleep in death!
Infernal horrors ſure will ſhake your ſoul
When o'er your head the awful thunders roll.
Earth cannot hide you, always will the cry
Of Murder! Murder! haunt you 'till you die!
To yonder grave! with trembling joints repair,
Remember, SEIDER's corps lies mould'ring there;
There drop a tear, and think what you have done!
Then judge how you can live beneath the Sun.
A PARDON may arrive! You laws defy,
But Heaven's laws will ſtand when KINGS ſhall die.
Oh! Wretched man! the monſter of the times,
You were not hung "by reaſon of *old* Lines,"+
Old Lines thrown by, 'twas then we were in hopes,
That you would ſoon be hung with *new made* Ropes *
But neither *Ropes nor Lines*, will ſatisfiy
For SEIDER's blood! But GOD is ever nigh,
And guilty ſouls will not unpuniſh'd go
Tho' they're excus'd by judges here below!
You are enlarg'd but curſed is your fate
Tho' †*Cuſhing*'s eas'd you from the priſon gate
The ‡*Bridge* of *Tories*, *it* has borne you o'er
Yet you e'er long may meet with HELL's dark ſhore.

+ "Lines" – the name of one of the Judges
* Name of another Judge
† Do: of another of the Judges
‡ Trowbridge another Judge

genuinely hated the British and their agents. He had grown up hearing angry words about the taxation of Boston's trade with the outside world. He probably remembered seeing angry crowds storming through the streets protesting the Stamp Act of 1765. Later, he had seen British soldiers in their red coats challenging peaceable citizens on the night streets and brawling with the town's toughs at the least excuse. But now Christopher Seider lay dying, and his reasons for joining the crowd made little difference.

The crowd went crazy, smashing the front door and charging inside to find Ebenezer Richardson. Men shouted for a rope and glanced around for a suitable tree to hang the villain. Then a loud voice called for calm. William Molineux, a well-known patriot, separated the terrified Richardson from his captors. There must be a trial, not lynch-mob justice in Boston, Molineux announced. Unwillingly, the crowd agreed.

More blood would flow in the city's streets before Richardson came to trial in the spring. He was convicted of murder but then pardoned by the king. Newspapers throughout the colonies denounced the king's action. The ties that bound America to Britain were fraying. The final break was yet years

The colonists were enraged by the shooting of eleven-year-old Christopher Seider by Ebenezer Richardson. This broadside, accuses Richardson of murder and condemns him to hell.

away, but more and more people began talking quietly of what had seemed unimaginable not long before—revolution.

Britannia Rules

A decade earlier, the ties between Britain and the thirteen American colonies had never seemed stronger. On both sides of the Atlantic, there were celebrations of Britain's stunning victories over the French in America, Europe, the Caribbean, and India. Britain's most glorious triumph in the Seven Years' War—called the French and Indian War in America—had been the taking of France's great fortress city of Quebec, a few hundred miles north of Boston. The loss of Quebec ended France's long rule in Canada and seemed to assure a British future for North America.

Colonial troops had fought alongside regular British soldiers in many of the battles in North America, and the colonies welcomed the prospect of peace after seventy years of on-and-off-again conflict with the French. Without French warships to dodge, the expert seafarers of the colonies anticipated a busy and profitable trade in the Caribbean, Africa, and Europe. Without the French to arm and incite the Indians, pioneers expected little opposition in the vast wilderness west of the Appalachian Mountains.

However, the government in London saw the future somewhat differently. Victory over France had cost a great deal of money. The expanded British Empire needed more funds and better management. It was time for the American colonies to start paying their fair share of the empire's expenses and obeying the rules—particularly those involving settlement and trade—laid down by the "mother country" for the good of her children.

Mother and Children

In the years before the Revolution, many a writer and speaker described the problems between Britain and the thirteen colonies in terms of the relationship between a mother and her children. What freedoms did the mother country owe its colonies? What obedience did the colonies owe the mother country? These were hardly easy questions—and honest people often reached opposite conclusions—but the dispute in its simplest terms *was* very like the squabbles found in nearly every family with growing children.

The American colonies felt they had grown to a responsible young adulthood. They accepted that the mother country should set policy for the empire's relationship with rival nations, and they would, of course, stand behind Britain in case of war. Otherwise, the colonies did not want to be mothered, but allowed to make most of their own decisions about future growth and development.

Britain saw the colonies not as young adults, but as unruly adolescents needing more, not less, guidance than before. To repay the generosity heaped on them in their infancy, the colonies should put aside their selfish ambitions and work for the good of the empire as a whole. At the head of the imperial family, Britain would continue to play the role of the firm, loving, and very-much-in-charge mother.

Ruling an Empire

The British Empire was united—at least in theory—by loyalty to the king of England. Unlike most of the world's monarchs in 1760, the king of England was not an absolute ruler. In the seventeenth century, the people of England had risen twice in rebellion, executing one king and deposing another. Later kings had had to tread lightly. Although a king could still exercise considerable influence, a legislature called Parliament held the majority of power.

The people of England, Scotland, and Wales (together referred to as Great Britain) were represented in the two houses of Parliament. The House of Lords consisted of members of the nobility and bishops of the Church of England. The House of Commons was made up of representatives elected by the common people. Although the right to vote was restricted to landowners, the people of Britain had more say in their government than almost any people on earth.

Parliament passed laws and levied taxes. From its ranks, the king chose a prime minister to conduct the day-to-day administration of the empire. The prime minister selected other ministers to run the departments of government. The prime minister had to maintain good relations with Parliament, which held the empire's purse strings, and with the king, who could dismiss him.

In 1760, the empire crowned a new king, George III, a not very bright but honest and sincere young man of twenty-two. He was particularly interested in eliminating corruption in government and restoring the financial health of the empire. These were fine goals, but George III was not skillful in their pursuit. He was stubborn to the point of pigheadedness and rarely able

England's George III at age twenty-three. The American colonists came to perceive him as a tyrant.

to see any other side to an argument but his own. A stronger, more able king might have guided his empire better. But, like his ministers, King George had little sympathy for the problems and dreams of the colonies.

The Thriving Colonies

The thirteen colonies were prosperous and energetic in 1760. The colonies had swelled in population from about seventy-five thousand non-Indian residents to some 1.6 million people in a century. In the next fifteen years, the population would increase by another million.

Blacks—almost all of them slaves—made up about a fifth of the population. The vast majority of the white colonists were of English, Scotch, Scotch-Irish, or Irish ancestry. In the Hudson River Valley of New York, there was a large Dutch community, and a sizeable number of Germans had settled in Pennsylvania and Virginia. A dozen other nationalities and races, including Jews, Swedes, Finns, Belgians, and French, were represented in smaller numbers.

The English-speaking majority felt quite comfortable with the colonies' membership in the British Empire. The British army and navy provided security. The English constitution and law provided a framework for an orderly society. The colonists shared—or at least believed they shared—those "sacred rights of Englishmen" that gave the people of Britain a freedom all but unknown elsewhere.

Except for the black slaves, Americans were truly one of the freest peoples in the world. For decades the colonies had been largely self-governing. Most white males had the right to vote for representatives to the colonial assemblies. The king ap-

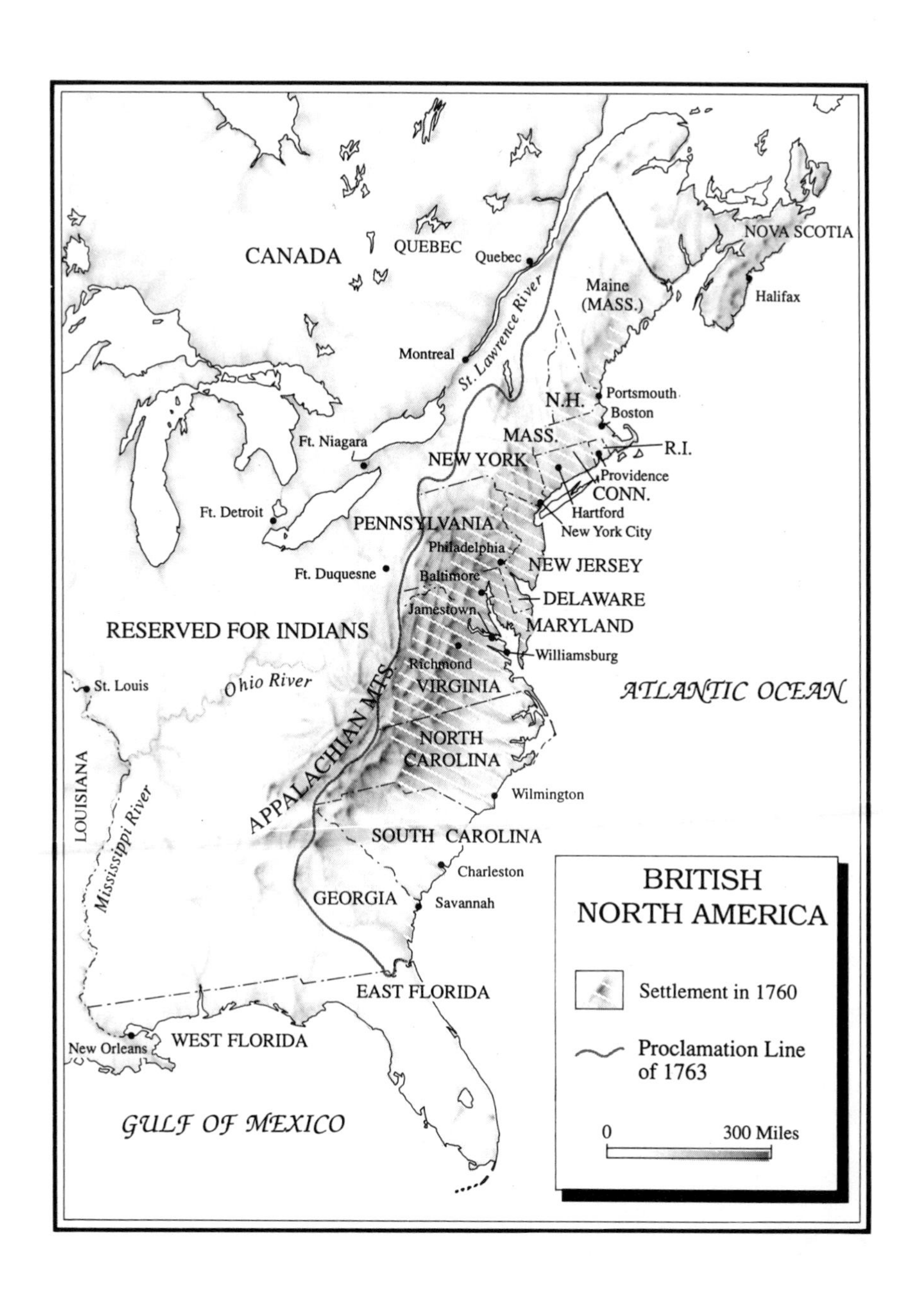
CANADA
QUEBEC
Quebec
NOVA SCOTIA
Halifax
Maine
(MASS.)
St. Lawrence River
Montreal
N.H.
Portsmouth
Boston
MASS.
R.I.
Ft. Niagara
NEW YORK
Providence
CONN.
Hartford
New York City
Ft. Detroit
PENNSYLVANIA
Philadelphia
NEW JERSEY
Ft. Duquesne
Baltimore
DELAWARE
Jamestown
MARYLAND
RESERVED FOR INDIANS
Williamsburg
Richmond
St. Louis
Ohio River
VIRGINIA
ATLANTIC OCEAN
APPALACHIAN MTS.
NORTH
CAROLINA
LOUISIANA
Mississippi River
Wilmington
SOUTH CAROLINA
Charleston
GEORGIA
Savannah
EAST FLORIDA
New Orleans
WEST FLORIDA
GULF OF MEXICO
BRITISH
NORTH AMERICA
Settlement in 1760
Proclamation Line
of 1763
0
300 Miles

proved governors for all the colonies except Connecticut and Rhode Island, where the assemblies elected their own. Friction was common between the royal governors and the assemblies; however, through control of taxation, the assemblies held the advantage most of the time.

Colonial assemblies were spirited gatherings, rarely resolving any problem without considerable and often hot debate. Between sessions, issues were vigorously argued in print. Most newspapers were controlled by political groups, or factions, more interested in promoting their cause than seeking the truth. No wonder that more than one frustrated royal governor wrote home complaining that Americans had much passion but little talent for self-government.

In dealing with the assemblies, royal governors usually had to depend on their wits rather than instructions from home. A letter took an average of eight weeks to reach London, four thousand miles across the Atlantic. Once there, it might lie unanswered for months. Several ministries divided responsibility for colonial policy. To this confusion was added the government's customary lack of interest in the internal affairs of the colonies. With little support or direction from London, the wiser royal governors rarely tried to dictate to the assemblies, and the colonies went pretty much their own way.

Town meetings in the colonies were spirited gatherings as differences of opinion over government policies often led to heated arguments.

An Ambitious People

In 1760, most colonists were too busy with their lives to worry much about the problems of the empire. Many visitors from Europe commented on the bustling activity of the colonial cities. People seemed more in a hurry, less concerned about ancient customs and class distinctions. In the colonies, ambition and intelligence meant more than who a person's parents were or where he had gone to school. Benjamin Franklin, America's most famous man, had started his career as an apprentice printer with little money or formal education. If a poor boy like Franklin could become a world famous scientist, inventor, philosopher, and public servant, then why not the next man?

Like most societies of the day, colonial America was dominated by white males. Few girls went to school, and women did not have the right to vote. Yet even women had more rights and opportunities in America. Sarah Kemble Knight lived a life of self-reliance as a teacher and innkeeper, leaving behind a journal that provides some of our best insights into colonial life. The lively and intelligent Abigail Adams had great influence with her husband John, one of the most important revolutionary leaders and later the country's second president.

A Growing Sense of Unity

Well before the Revolution, the colonies were drawing closer together. One of Franklin's major achievements was the design of an efficient postal service linking the colonies. In the 1750s, mail between Philadelphia and New York was delivered in thirty-six hours. Eventually, colonial post roads stretched from St. Augustine in Florida to Falmouth, in present-day Maine, with a branch line from New York City to Montreal.

The improved communications encouraged the feeling that the colonies shared more with each other than with the distant mother country. In 1754, delegates from seven of the colonies met in Albany, New York, to discuss relations with the Indians. Franklin persuaded the Albany Congress to pass a resolution calling for the unification of the colonies. However, several colonial assemblies did not share the congress's spirit of unity and rejected the resolution. The British government also disliked the idea, preferring to keep the colonies divided and weak. Yet, despite the failure of Franklin's plan, a movement toward unity had begun.

Americans were intensely interested in the news from other colonies. Every arriving postal rider and ship's crewman was questioned. The colonies' scores of small newspapers carried the latest news brought by land or sea. The newspapers themselves were widely circulated. It was not uncommon for a Boston paper to find its way to Savannah in less than three weeks—a very short time in the eighteenth century.

Colonial Commerce

Although Americans were deeply interested in politics, they focused the main part of their energies on making a decent living. A sizeable majority of the colonists were farmers. In all, some ninety percent of the people lived on farms or in country villages. The villages provided markets for farm produce, shops selling goods that could not be made at home, and the services of blacksmiths, wheelwrights, and other skilled craftsmen.

On the outskirts of civilization, fur trapping, lumbering, and the production of naval stores—the pitch, turpentine, and rosin used in shipbuilding—were major industries. Shipbuilding

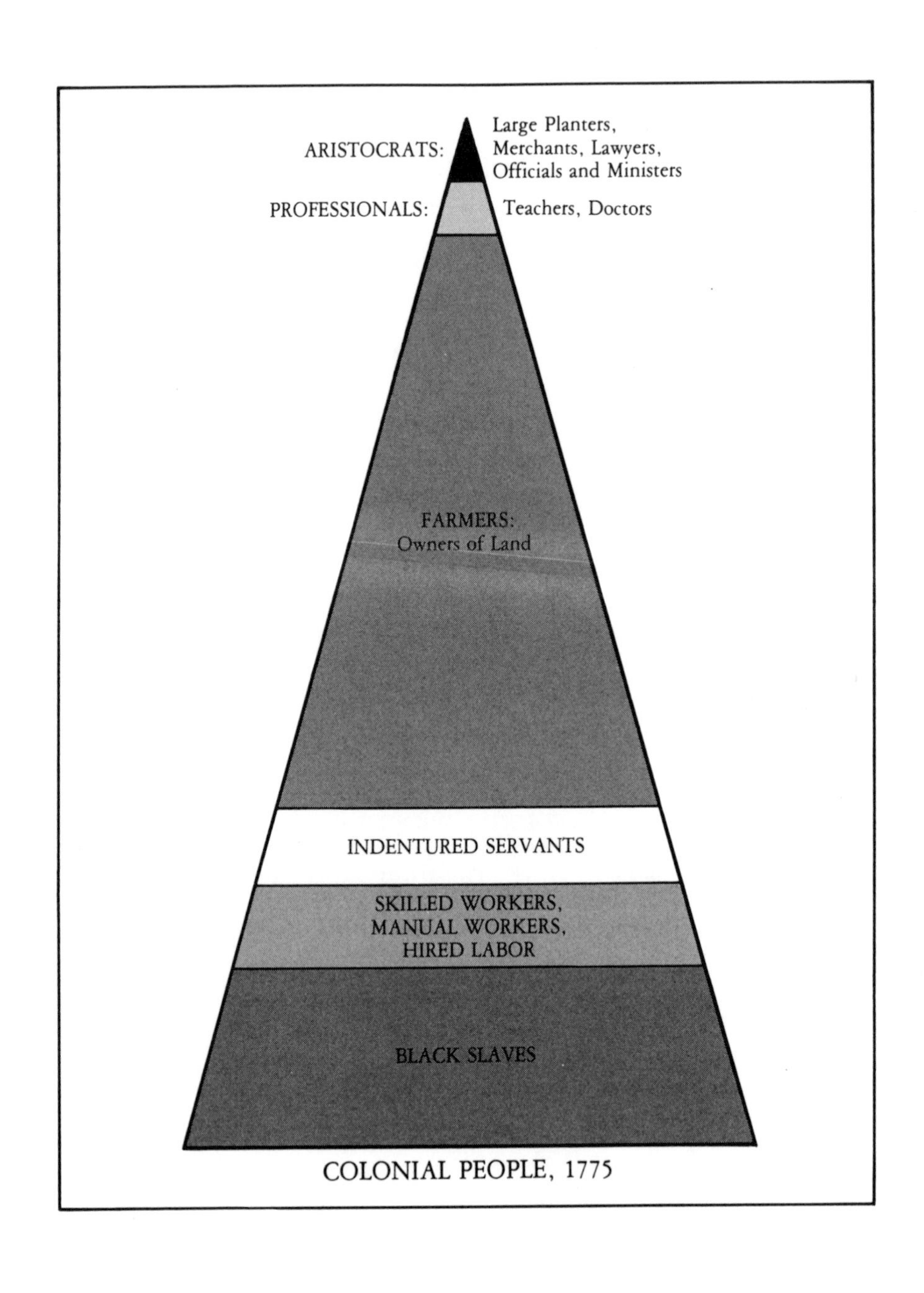

COLONIAL PEOPLE, 1775

thrived along the coast, particularly in New England. With the exception of a fair number of ironworks, the colonies had few factories. Thousands of ships loaded raw materials in colonial seaports and then set sail for Europe, to return months later with cargoes of manufactured goods.

Most farms in the New England colonies—Massachusetts, New Hampshire, Connecticut, and Rhode Island—were small and could be worked by a single family. Few slaves lived in the region, since most New Englanders considered slavery immoral and had little need for slave labor anyway. Grain and cattle were the major agricultural products. Some hides and meat were shipped to Europe, but most produce was consumed within New England. Far more important as an export was the rum made in New England from imported sugar.

New England's ships and sailors were among the world's best. Yankee fishermen ventured far into the icy waters of the North Atlantic for cod, much of their catch eventually landing on the supper tables of Europe. Nantucket and New Bedford, Massachusetts, were the home ports of whaling fleets. Portsmouth, New Hampshire, was the major loading point for straight pine logs destined to stand as masts on colonial merchant ships or the warships of the British navy. Merchant ships from such ports as Providence and Newport, Rhode Island, and New Haven and New London, Connecticut, sailed the coastal waters of the thirteen colonies or set out across the Atlantic for Europe and Africa. Boston dwarfed all the other ports of New England. The largest city with the busiest harbor, Boston attracted influence and—as events would soon show—trouble.

The Middle Atlantic colonies of New York, Pennsylvania, New Jersey, Delaware, and Maryland boasted larger farms and more agricultural exports. New York City and Baltimore, Maryland,

Above: a view of the great port of Boston in the 1730s

Right: tobacco was the single most important export of the thirteen colonies. This picture of tobacco merchants on a wharf is from a map of Virginia and Maryland published in London in 1751.

rivaled Boston as centers of trade and learning. With forty thousand residents by 1775, Philadelphia, Pennsylvania, was the largest and most sophisticated city in the colonies.

From Maryland south, the character of colonial agriculture changed. The economies of Maryland, Delaware, and the southern colonies of Virginia and North Carolina depended on the growing of tobacco. Some of America's first European explorers had learned tobacco's use from the Indians, and the "noxious weed" had become the single most important export of the thirteen colonies.

Most of the tobacco crop was grown on large plantations with the use of slave labor. In South Carolina and Georgia, slave labor was also vital to the cultivation of rice and indigo, a plant producing a valuable blue dye. The plantation owners enjoyed a life of ease and luxury almost unknown farther north. However, small farmers in the region's western counties were among the poorest citizens of the thirteen colonies.

The southern colonies had few large cities. Norfolk, Richmond, and Williamsburg in Virginia, and Wilmington and New Bern in North Carolina were thriving towns. Charleston was South Carolina's major city and port. Savannah, Georgia, was the southernmost city of importance in the colonies.

A Clash of Expectations

In the peace immediately following the victory over France, Britain and the prosperous American colonies seemed securely bound by a common heritage, thriving trade, and a loyalty to king and empire. Yet Britain and the colonies had different visions of the future. This clash of expectations would lead to angry exchanges, rioting, and eventually war.

No Taxation without Representation

The era of good feeling between Britain and the colonies did not last long. Shortly after signing a peace treaty with France, the British government issued the Proclamation of 1763, forbidding all settlement west of the Appalachians. Soon afterward, word arrived in the colonies that Parliament had passed a strong new law, the Sugar Act of 1764, to regulate colonial trade.

In London's view, the proclamation and the Sugar Act were entirely reasonable policies, but the colonies reacted with dismay and anger. Was this the reward they deserved for loyally supporting the empire in its war with France? Had some plot been hatched in London to deprive the colonies of their promising future?

Restricting Settlement

Worried about trouble with the Indians, the government had been trying to restrict the spread of settlement for several years. In the spring of 1763, a great uprising by the Indians confirmed

Britain's fears. Inspired by the Ottawa chief Pontiac, the Indians ravaged the frontier. Colonial militiamen and British regulars marched into the wilderness to begin a three-year campaign to restore peace.

The Proclamation of 1763 was designed to give the government time to gain control of the vast lands won from France. The French had followed a policy of discouraging settlement in the American interior while gathering the wealth of the region with a small army of fur traders. The French relationship with the Indians had been profitable and peaceful. The British government decided to continue the French policy for the immediate future. To protect the frontier and to give work to battle-hardened troops, the government decided to station regular army units permanently in the colonies.

The new policy outraged many colonists. Some settlers in western Pennsylvania and Virginia had been living beyond the Appalachians for twenty years or more. They had fled east when Pontiac's Rebellion erupted and would be forbidden to return under the new law. Thousands of new immigrants were poised for the journey west. Ambitious men, including Benjamin Franklin and a young Virginian named George Washington, were shareholders in companies promoting settlement. Their investments would be worthless under the proclamation.

Soon colonists were openly disobeying the proclamation. Farmers returned to their abandoned homes. New pioneers chopped farms out of the wilderness. Trading companies set up shop as far inland as the Illinois country. The thin line of British troops along the frontier could do little but remove or turn back an occasional settler or trader—actions which further embittered the colonists.

Many colonists who had no intention of becoming pioneers were alarmed by the government's decision to station a regular army in the colonies. Most people felt that the militias raised in the colonies were more than strong enough to deal with the Indians. Militiamen were neighbors and friends, their senior officers approved by the colonial assemblies. Regular army troops would be professionals under the command of officers accountable only to the British government. Regulars could be used to enforce unpopular laws and put down protests.

Regulating Trade

The British government paid little attention to colonial complaints. The prime minister, George Grenville, was far more interested in the financial health of the empire. Britain's war debts were huge, and the expense of running the expanded empire—including the maintenance of troops in America—promised to be large. The Sugar Act of 1764 was an attempt to impose order on colonial trade and collect the taxes colonial traders had been neglecting to pay.

For more than a century, the British Empire had operated on the mercantile theory. In simple terms, the theory stated that colonies existed for the economic benefit of the mother country. The theory was made law by the Navigation Acts. The colonies were to send raw materials to Britain and receive manufactured goods in return. All exports and imports had to be carried in British or colonial ships. All cargoes were subject to taxes called tariffs or duties. If a colonial merchant wanted to export a product to any country besides Britain, he had to order his ship to stop first at a British-owned port to pay duties. The same held true for the return voyage. Even trade between the colonies was subject to duties. To enforce the Navigation Acts, the government created a customs service whose agents inspected cargoes and determined the duties due.

The Navigation Acts contained benefits for the colonies. Tariffs on colonial exports to Britain were usually reasonable and almost always lower than those paid by traders from foreign countries. The government paid a bonus for the production of indigo and naval stores. Virginia enjoyed a particularly profitable trade since the acts forbade the growing of tobacco in Britain.

However, as the colonies grew, the Navigation Acts became increasingly unfair. By the middle of the eighteenth century, many of the rules were outdated and costly to obey. To make matters worse, the customs service was inefficient and corrupt. Its principal agents often lived in England and sent low-paid assistants to America. Many of the agents in the colonies regularly accepted money from merchants who considered bribery little more than a necessary business expense. Other merchants avoided both duties and bribes by unloading their ships at night or in small out-of-the-way ports. Illegal trade with foreign nations was commonplace. It particularly angered the government that colonial merchants secretly traded with France throughout the long wars.

Molasses and Slaves

The Sugar Act of 1764 actually covered a number of products, but the tax on sugar touched a sore spot for colonial merchants. Sugar was a critical item in what was called the triangular trade. Sugar was imported in the form of molasses from the West Indian islands of the Caribbean in exchange for fish, meat, lumber, and other colonial products. The molasses was converted to rum by New England distilleries. Much of the rum was then shipped to Africa where it was exchanged for slaves. The slave ships sailed back across the Atlantic to offload their

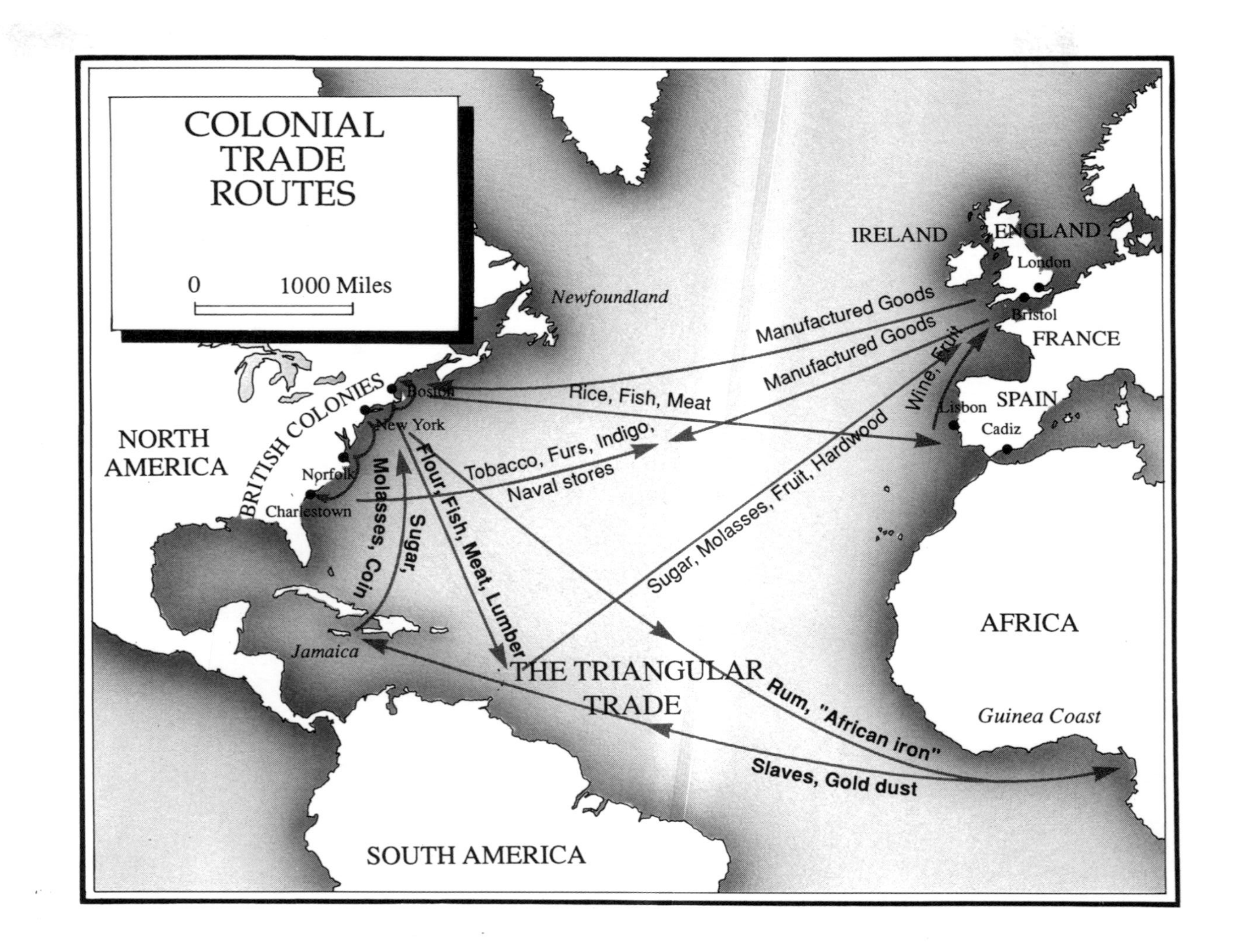
COLONIAL TRADE ROUTES
0
1000 Miles
Newfoundland
IRELAND
ENGLAND
London
Bristol
FRANCE
SPAIN
Lisbon
Cadiz
NORTH AMERICA
BRITISH COLONIES
Boston
New York
Norfolk
Charlestown
Manufactured Goods
Manufactured Goods
Rice, Fish, Meat
Wine, Fruit
Tobacco, Furs, Indigo,
Naval stores
Sugar, Molasses, Fruit, Hardwood
Sugar,
Molasses, Coin
Flour, Fish, Meat, Lumber
Jamaica
THE TRIANGULAR TRADE
Rum, "African iron"
Slaves, Gold dust
AFRICA
Guinea Coast
SOUTH AMERICA

human cargoes in the West Indies or the southern colonies. Many of the ships then picked up barrels of molasses to bring back to New England.

The slave trade was horrible in its cost in human life and liberty. Yet its immorality was ignored by both the colonial merchants and the British ministers. The colonial complaint was that the British-owned islands in the West Indies did not produce enough low-duty sugar to keep the trade going. The colonies must also import sugar from the French- and Dutch-held islands. The high duty on foreign molasses increased the expense of making rum, and decreased profits.

Actually, the tariff imposed by the Sugar Act was a reduction from the earlier duty, but Prime Minister Grenville was determined that colonial traders would pay it this time. He ordered British naval vessels to colonial waters to help in enforcement. He conducted a reorganization of the customs service, ordering all of its colonial collectors to the colonies. (A number of them resigned rather than abandon the comfortable life in Britain.)

Most threatening of the new customs regulations was the provision that violators could be tried in vice-admiralty courts run by the British navy. Colonial courts usually treated customs violators sympathetically, but a defendant entering a vice-admiralty court was presumed guilty and had to prove his innocence.

Rebellion in the Soul

The reaction in the colonies to Grenville's hard-nosed policies revealed something that he and probably most colonists had forgotten—rebellion came naturally to Americans. The majority of the original white settlers had come to the New World because they were dissatisfied with life in Europe. They had fled religious persecution, poverty, war, and a class system that kept a few people rich and the great majority poor. Even many wealthy Virginia planters could trace their family trees to unhappy younger sons of well-to-do English families. Under English law, all a father's property was left to his eldest son, and younger sons had to seek careers in the army, navy, church, or the New World.

Common in the background of virtually all the colonists—and many more were arriving yearly—was a desire for individual liberty and opportunity. When the distant government in London began interfering, an angry reaction was inevitable.

No Taxation Without Representation

The colonial merchants organized to protest the Sugar Act. By the fall of 1764, nine colonial assemblies had sent messages to London. The common argument was that the government misunderstood the complexities of colonial trade. However, two assemblies, New York's and North Carolina's, raised a different point. They maintained that Britain had no right to impose taxes on the colonies because the colonies had no elected representation in Parliament.

The principle that taxes could be levied only with the consent of the people had long been accepted in Britain as one of the "sacred rights of Englishmen." Yet Parliament seemed to be saying that the principle no longer held in the colonies, where previously only the assemblies had levied taxes.

As applied to the Sugar Act, the "no taxation without representation" argument was flimsy. The Sugar Act was not much different from laws that had been passed before, and it applied only to international trade, an area where Parliament had usually done what it liked. Indeed, the Sugar Act might have been grudgingly accepted by the colonies had the government not set about its enforcement with such heavy-handed thoroughness.

Naval officers in particular often lacked both politeness and honesty when enforcing customs regulations. Parliament had not intended for the new rules to apply to small coastal vessels, but British officers seized them anyway. Following a longstanding tradition, the navy then sold the ships and cargoes at auction—with much of the profit ending up in its officers' pockets.

Fighting Back

The merchants fought back, finding willing allies among sailors and other workingmen in the port cities. The Royal Navy was already widely disliked by the working class. To gain sailors for its ships, the navy often resorted to "impressment." Led by tough petty officers, "press gangs" would roam the narrow streets near a colonial city's harbor. A drunken sailor staggering down an alley or a tradesman hurrying home from his shop might feel a blow behind his ear and wake in the morning to find himself at sea, a member of the British navy.

The Sugar Act gave workingmen an excuse to strike back. Brawls between British sailors and tough colonials broke out in a number of ports. In New York, an informer for the customs service was paraded through the streets and pelted with filth by a mob. Off Newport, a British boarding party and a colonial crew fought with swords and axes. In Dighton, Massachusetts, the sloop *Polly* was seized by an honest customs inspector, John Robinson. While Robinson was in Newport recruiting a new crew, an angry crowd retook the ship, offloaded its cargo of molasses, and sank the *Polly* to prevent it from falling into the hands of the auctioneer. On his return, Robinson was informed by the local sheriff that the *Polly*'s owner was suing for the loss of ship and cargo. Robinson spent the next two days in a jail cell, by all accounts unable to see the humor in his predicament.

A more serious incident occurred in Newport. Crew members of a small British naval vessel, the *St. John,* were accused of kidnapping civilians to man the ship. When the *St. John* sailed out of port, colonial officials ordered the harbor's cannon to fire on the ship. There were no hits and the *St. John* kept going, but a dangerous point had been reached: shots had been fired with the official permission of colonial leaders.

The Stamp Act

Despite the uproar, the situation still might have cooled had the British government not blundered by imposing another tax at the worst possible time. The Proclamation of 1763 and the Sugar Act of 1764 had directly affected only a small number of colonists; the Stamp Act of 1765 taxed nearly everyone. The Stamp Act required that all newspapers, bills of sale, pamphlets, legal documents, advertisements, and numerous other papers must carry a stamp sold by the government. Besides raising money, the Stamp Act also made it possible for the customs service to keep track of colonial trade.

The Stamp Act represented the first attempt by Parliament to tax the internal business of the colonies. There could be no doubt that the colonies' "no taxation without representation" argument applied to the Stamp Act. But more than money was involved for the colonists. The power of a colonial assembly rested on its control of internal taxation. If the British government won the right to impose these taxes, then a royal governor would have little reason to call a colony's assembly into session. With British regulars to back him up, a governor would become a virtual dictator.

The Virginia assembly, the House of Burgesses, was the first to denounce the Stamp Act. Late in May—when most of its members had already gone home—a young lawyer and fiery orator, Patrick Henry, introduced a set of resolutions, or resolves, opposing the interference of Parliament in colonial affairs. Although the cautious representatives toned down the language of Henry's draft before approving it, the Virginia Resolves had a striking effect. Widely—and often inaccurately—reprinted in the newspapers, the resolves familiarized the public with the "no taxation without representation" argument. By the end of 1765, eight other colonial legislatures would pass similar appeals to the king.

In October of 1765, nine of the colonies sent representatives to New York City for the Stamp Act Congress. The first colonial congress since the Albany Congress more than a decade before, the Stamp Act Congress gave the colonies a chance to show their unified opposition to Prime Minister Grenville's policies.

The Sons of Liberty

The Stamp Act caused widespread protests in the summer and fall of 1765. Throughout the colonies, angry citizens marched on the homes of the government's stamp distributors. The protesters often burned wood and paper statues, called effigies, of stamp distributors and government ministers. Afraid for their lives and property, almost all the stamp distributors resigned.

The protest turned violent in Boston, where full-scale rioting broke out. Behind much of the violence was a recently formed group of radicals who called themselves the Sons of

Liberty. Their leader was Samuel Adams. Despite intelligence and a good education, Adams had been unsuccessful at several occupations before discovering a flair for politics. A skilled writer and talented leader, Adams was one of the first prominent men in the colonies to favor separation from the British Empire. In the next decade, probably no one else would have greater influence in colonial events.

Adams and the Sons of Liberty organized the tougher elements of Boston's population and led them in attacks on the homes of stamp distributors, customs agents, and other officials thought friendly to Parliament's policies. In one riot, a mob literally tore down the mansion of Judge Thomas Hutchinson, who had spent his life serving his native Massachusetts.

To communicate with radical groups in other colonies, the Sons of Liberty formed a "committee of correspondence." The Boston committee argued for a boycott of British goods. By refusing to buy or sell imports from Britain, the colonists could hit the British merchants where it hurt most—in the pocketbook. Most colonial merchants lent their support to the boycott, and by late fall, trade between Britain and the colonies was taking a beating. The merchants of Britain set up a howl.

Repeal and Its Consequences

In Parliament, the complaints of the British merchants brought calls for the repeal of the Stamp Act. A few members of Parliament even argued that the colonies were correct in denouncing the tax as unfair and a violation of the English constitution. By this time Grenville had been replaced by a new prime minister, Lord Rockingham. Rockingham maneuvered a repeal through Parliament early in 1766.

In 1765, The Stamp Act inflamed colonial resentment. Here, Boston's citizens burn Stamp Act papers in protest.

The Sons of Liberty, a group of radicals, protesting what they believed to be unfair taxation, tar and feather a tax collector.

Upon the repeal of the Stamp Act, this privately minted token was issued, celebrating the repeal and paying tribute to America's good friend William Pitt. The legend around the profile of Pitts reads, "The Restorer of Commerce 1766, No Stamps." On the reverse side are the words, "Thanks to the Friends of Liberty and Trade."

News of the Stamp Act's repeal was greeted with wild celebration in America. Most colonists thought that they had backed down the British lion—and in a way they had—but Parliament remained determined to bring the colonies to heel. Little noticed by the colonies was a new law passed at the same time as the repeal. The Declaratory Act stated that Parliament had the power to pass laws "to bind the colonies in all cases whatsoever." In other words, Parliament—even in its moment of defeat on the Stamp Act—was stating flatly that it possessed unlimited powers over the colonies.

In the colonies, the Stamp Act Crisis had several important consequences. Colonial leaders would remain in correspondence, sharing ideas and developing a sense of common purpose. The colonial denial of Parliament's right to tax was now popularly accepted. The radical factions favoring maximum freedom of action for the colonies had gained power over the more conservative elements in the assemblies. Perhaps most important, the colonies had demonstrated their ability to stand together in a crisis. They would need that spirit of unity again—and very soon.

Parliament Strikes Back

After the violence of the Stamp Act riots, Parliament should have reexamined its attitude toward America. No deep hatreds yet divided mother country and colonies. Compromise, fairness, and attention to colonial complaints might have repaired the damage. Instead, Parliament came down hard on the colonies.

The Quartering Act

Even before the repeal of the Stamp Act, another dispute was brewing. In the midst of the crisis, Parliament passed the Quartering Act of 1765. The law stated that it was a colonial responsibility to provide living quarters and certain supplies for regular army troops stationed in America.

Most of these soldiers had been serving on the frontier since Pontiac's Rebellion in 1763. During the Stamp Act Crisis, they were ordered back East, most of them to the Hudson River Valley of New York. The New York assembly viewed the troops as a threat to its independence. Furthermore, the Quartering

Act seemed yet another attempt by the British government to impose a tax. The assembly refused to pay for the upkeep of the soldiers. General Thomas Gage, a patient and highly professional soldier, presented the list of expenses several times before appealing to London in the winter of 1766.

The Townshend Acts

Gage's complaint found a willing listener in Charles Townshend, an ambitious young minister in the government of William Pitt, Earl of Chatham, who had succeeded Rockingham as prime minister the previous summer. Pitt was a national hero. As prime minister in the late 1750s, he had led Britain to victory in the war with France. He was sympathetic to the colonies and had argued the colonial side of the taxation issue in Parliament. But he was now old, sick, and depressed. He left his cabinet ministers to run the government, while he tried to regain his health and spirits away from London.

Brilliant and forceful, Townshend became the most powerful man in the government. He pushed for a new series of laws to strengthen royal power in America. He argued that royal officials must be freed from dependence on colonial assemblies for their salaries and expenses. Without control of the purse strings, the power of the assemblies would evaporate, leaving the royal governors free to rule the colonies according to the will of Parliament.

News of the New York assembly's disobedience helped to secure Parliament's approval of the Townshend Acts early in the summer of 1767. The acts imposed a tariff on lead, glass, paint, paper, and tea. The duties would be collected by a powerful new commission, the American Board of Customs Commissioners, and used to pay the salaries of colonial officials.

Parliament also threatened to suspend the New York assembly and deny it the right to meet again unless it obeyed the Quartering Act.

Angry Reaction

The colonists reacted to news of the Townshend Acts with disappointment, confusion, and anger. They thought they had made their point during the Stamp Act Crisis, and yet here was another attempt to impose taxes on the colonies. Townshend died suddenly in September, unaware of the lasting damage his work would do.

By the time the first snows fell in the colonies, the temperature of colonial anger was rising fast. In New York, the assembly had caved in and agreed to pay the army's expenses, but relations between soldiers and common citizens worsened anyway. Most British soldiers had escaped to the army from the lowest levels of society. Magnificently disciplined on the battlefield, they were often rough, impolite, and rowdy when off-duty. On the streets of New York City, the soldiers found ready enemies in tough sailors, tradesmen, apprentices, and laborers. Scuffles and brawls broke out. The New York Sons of Liberty encouraged the unrest, and full-scale rioting threatened.

Official colonial reaction to the Townshend Acts came first from the Massachusetts assembly. In February 1768, the assembly sent a "circular letter" to the other colonial assemblies, calling for united opposition to the acts. The wording adopted by the assembly was milder than such leading radicals as Sam Adams and James Otis might have wished. However, many people—particularly influential merchants—feared a repetition of the Stamp Act riots and trade boycott.

Mild words were not, however, common in the battle soon

In a sympathetic British cartoon, a tax collector points a gun at the colonists and demands money. King George III stands at the right. He is saying, "Necessity pinches me, money we must have."

raging in the Massachusetts assembly and the Boston newspapers. The royal governor, Francis Bernard, and the Otis–Adams faction hurled threats and insults at each other. By engaging in the conflict, Bernard, a man of little brainpower but immense pride, only made a bad situation worse. On the anniversary of the Stamp Act's repeal, thousands of protesters marched through the streets, burning the governor's effigy and taunting the customs agents.

The Liberty Incident

The newly created American Board of Customs Commissioners pushed a tough program of customs collection. For the commissioners, more than money was at stake; they were out to crush colonial disobedience.

The customs commissioners decided to make an example of one of Boston's leading foes of the customs service, the wealthy merchant John Hancock. On June 10, 1768, they ordered Hancock's sloop *Liberty* seized for a minor customs violation. Sailors from the fifty-gun warship *Romney* assisted the customs agents, fighting briefly with some of Hancock's supporters before towing the *Liberty* away from the wharf.

The Sons of Liberty took the opportunity to show their muscle. Angry demonstrators swept through Boston. For several days, the Sons of Liberty controlled Boston before allowing Governor Bernard to reassert his tattered authority. The Sons of Liberty had made their point: they could take over anytime they wanted to.

The Assemblies Suspended

As news of the struggle in Boston spread, colonial assemblies began responding to the Massachusetts circular letter. By late spring, New Jersey and Connecticut had replied favorably, and Virginia was circulating an even stronger letter.

The British government sent blunt instructions to Governor Bernard: the Massachusetts assembly must withdraw its letter or be suspended. Even Bernard was not stupid enough to think the assembly would agree, but he followed orders. The assembly refused, and Bernard ordered the members to go home.

The government had issued a challenge impossible for the other colonial assemblies to ignore. They rallied to the defense of Massachusetts. During the summer, almost all the assemblies passed resolutions supporting the Massachusetts circular letter. More than half of the assemblies were promptly suspended by their royal governors. The sacred right of Englishmen to meet freely and to send their complaints to the king no longer applied in the colonies.

The Occupation of Boston

A few months before, the colonists had been hesitant to begin another costly boycott of British imports. Now it seemed their best weapon, and a "nonimportation" campaign spread through the colonies. The boycott was strictly—sometimes savagely—enforced by the Sons of Liberty. As usual, unrest was greatest in Boston. Bernard requested troops to maintain order. At the end of September 1768, two regiments landed under the guns of a menacing line of warships.

Over the next year, Boston took on the grim aspect of a hostile city under military occupation. Armed patrols roamed the streets. Sentries challenged peaceable citizens for little or no reason. Small groups of men gathering quietly to discuss innocent matters were told to move on. Civilians reacted to the harassment by abusing the soldiers at every opportunity.

Governor Bernard—always more interested in money and prestige than responsibility—retired to England in August 1769. He was replaced by Lieutenant Governor Thomas Hutchinson. Hutchinson was a good man: intelligent, fair, brave, and dignified. When a mob had torn down his house in 1765 during the Stamp Act Crisis, a lesser man might have fled to England. But Hutchinson had stayed on, striving for a restoration of peace between Massachusetts and Britain. It was his fate to be the last civilian governor of the colony of Massachusetts.

The winter of 1769–1770 saw a renewal of violent demonstrations in several port cities. The Sons of Liberty were behind some of the outbreaks, while others simply happened. In New York, members of the Sons of Liberty put up a tall pole in the common, a park at the center of the city. This "Liberty tree" was supposed to provide a symbol for their cause and mark a meeting place for speeches. Soldiers cut it down, hacked it apart, and scattered the pieces in front of the headquarters of the Sons of Liberty. The insult touched off a three-day riot between soldiers and a mob estimated at three thousand. Scores were injured and one civilian killed.

In Boston, tension mounted. On February 22, young Christopher Seider became a martyr at the hands of Ebenezer Richardson. The Sons of Liberty gave the boy a huge funeral, marked by repeated calls for revenge. Brawls between soldiers and civilians and attacks on the homes of customs officials increased. Worse was to come.

Under a Cold Moon

The tragedy began beneath a late winter moon on the evening of March 5, 1770. Private Hugh White was standing sentry duty at the customhouse on King Street in Boston. A young apprentice passing in the street jeered that White's regiment contained "no gentlemen." Cold, tired, and long sick of the insults of Boston's citizens, White struck the young man with his musket.

It was a remarkably dangerous thing to do. A crowd gathered, cursing White and pelting him with snowballs. With his back against the customhouse wall, White stood his ground. At the guardhouse up the street, Captain Thomas Preston watched the scene uneasily, hoping the crowd would break up. He knew that if he intervened, he might touch off a riot.

Someone began to ring the bell of a nearby church. At an hour when no services were scheduled, the tolling brought many good citizens into the street to answer what they supposed was a call to fight a fire. As confusion and the size of the crowd grew, Preston decided that he must rescue White. He led a squad of seven soldiers down the street. They marched through the crowd to White and became—almost instantly—as much prisoners as the forlorn private.

For fifteen minutes the soldiers stood in a semicircle, their muskets pointed at the angry crowd. Shouts of "Kill them" came from the back of the mob. Boys ran down the line, clattering sticks against the line of bayonets. A prominent merchant, Richard Palmes, tried to calm the situation. While he was talking with Preston, someone in the crowd hurled a piece of ice that struck Private Hugh Montgomery. Montgomery staggered, regained his footing, and fired. There was a brief moment of silence as trigger fingers hesitated, then a ragged volley lashed into the crowd. There were screams, curses, and appeals to heaven—then a terrible reckoning of the dead and wounded. Three men had died instantly, two more lay mortally wounded, and six others bled from lesser injuries.

A 1770 engraving by Paul Revere, depicting the Boston Massacre. The first stanza of the poem reads, "Unhappy Boston! See thy Sons deplore, Thy hallow'd Walks besmear'd with guiltless gore, While faithless [Preston] and his savage Bands, With murd'rous Rancour stretch their bloody Hands, Like fierce Barbarians grinning o'er their Prey, Approve the Carnage and enjoy the Day."

Aftermath

Some would call it murder, others a tragic accident. History would call it the Boston Massacre. For the next day, the city was torn by rioting. Governor Hutchinson knew that open warfare could begin at any moment. He clapped Preston and his soldiers in jail, promising the people that a fair trial would follow. Then, in an act of extraordinary intelligence, he ordered the rest of the army from Boston. Revolution was avoided.

The authorities delayed the trial until the fall to give tempers time to cool. A cousin of the fiery Sam Adams, John Adams, stepped forward to conduct Preston's defense. John Adams was also a patriot and a Son of Liberty, but he believed every man deserved a fair trial. Preston and all but two of the soldiers were acquitted. The remaining two were convicted of manslaughter, branded on the thumb with a red hot iron—a painful but hardly severe or unusual punishment in the eighteenth century—and released.

Far away in London, more reasonable voices were at last being heard. Pitt's ministry was succeeded by yet another new government, this time under Lord Frederick North. The North ministry convinced Parliament to repeal the Townshend Acts. In the colonies, the boycott ended and the violence died down. Parliament kept only a modest duty on tea to demonstrate its right to tax the colonies. It would be enough to stir the pot again.

☆ 4 ☆

Bitter Tea

Despite their reputation in Britain, few colonial merchants were actually smugglers. Most merchants tried to operate within the law, even though the complexities of the Navigation Acts often left them at the mercy of nit-picking customs agents. Rhode Island merchants were an exception. In the smallest colony, smuggling had long been considered something between a good sport and a sacred right. Rhode Island became the scene of the next major incident in the struggle between Britain and America.

The Gaspee Incident

For the Royal Navy, policing the waters off Rhode Island was a frustrating task. Narragansett Bay, with its scores of sheltered coves, split the colony from the sea to Providence. Smugglers piloting their small fast vessels slipped in and out of the bay almost at will. Rhode Island was one of two colonies that elected its own governor, and the navy could count on little help from the civilian authorities in enforcing the customs regulations.

In late March 1772, the navy sent Lieutenant William Dudingston and his sloop, *Gaspee,* into the bay. Dudingston pursued smugglers with enthusiasm, soon earning the hatred of Rhode Islanders. On the night of June 9, Dudingston was lured into shallow waters by a fleeing smuggler. The *Gaspee* ran aground, and a large party of colonists boarded the ship. A fight left Dudingston lying wounded on the deck, his crew bruised and sullen, and the boarders in control. The colonists read the ship's papers, sent the crew ashore, then burned the *Gaspee.*

Dudingston's humiliation was just beginning. Two days later, the sheriff arrested the wounded officer for illegally seizing colonial vessels. Dudingston's admiral paid a large fine to free him, then packed him off to England to be court-martialed for losing his ship.

Governor Joseph Wanton issued a proclamation calling for the arrest of the boarders. Not surprisingly, none of the local heroes was arrested. The British government established a commission to investigate the incident, but it could find no informers to finger the boarders. The commission issued a mild report and dissolved itself.

Trial by One's Peers

The entire *Gaspee* affair might have gone down in history as mildly farcical—the fate of poor Dudingston notwithstanding—had it not been for one feature of the investigation. The government had given the commission the power to send suspects to England for trial. To the colonists, this represented the violation of yet one more of the "sacred rights of Englishmen."

Under the English constitution, any person accused of a crime had the right to a trial by an impartial jury of his fellow citizens, or peers. Hence, a colonial suspect could receive a fair trial only in the colonies by a jury of fellow colonists.

News of the latest violation of American rights spread through the colonies. For the first time, newspapers began discussing the possible advantages of independence. In Virginia, three very able men, Thomas Jefferson, Richard Henry Lee, and Patrick Henry, proposed that the House of Burgesses establish a permanent and formal committee of correspondence. Within a year, all the colonies except Pennsylvania had joined the network.

Stoking the Fires in Boston

The *Gaspee* incident gave Sam Adams an excuse to renew the struggle in Boston. At his suggestion, a Boston town meeting petitioned Governor Hutchinson to call a session of the Massachusetts assembly for the purpose of establishing a formal committee of correspondence. Hutchinson refused and lectured the town meeting on its limited rights.

Hutchinson was widely disliked and his lecture aroused anger. Adams fed the anger in the following months. He reminded the citizens that Hutchinson and a number of other officials were paid from the duty collected on tea. To make sure no one had forgotten the "no taxation without representation" argument, Adams and the local committee of correspondence issued a pamphlet. The authors concluded from the pattern of British actions that a plot existed to "enslave" the colonies. The Boston pamphlet said little new about the violation of colonial rights, but it was clearly written and very persuasive. Copies soon found their way as far south as Savannah.

The burning of the schooner Gaspee *off the coast of Rhode Island in 1772*

Parliament, with its customary sense of terrible timing, passed a new tea tax in the spring of 1773. The small duty remained the same, but a new regulation required that shipments could be delivered only to government-licensed importers called consignees.

By this time, it did not take much to heat colonial anger close to the boiling point. Newspapers were soon brimming with threats of action against the consignees. Angry mass meetings were held in Philadelphia and New York. Most of the cities' consignees quickly gave up their licenses. Tea ships arriving from India sat for a while at anchor, then sailed still fully loaded for England.

In Boston, Adams pointed out that one of the firms holding a consignment license was owned by the Hutchinson family. Despite the public outcry, the Hutchinson family and the other consignees refused to surrender their licenses.

Adams had a secret weapon to further embarrass the governor: a packet of letters written by Hutchinson to a British subminister. The letters had been acquired mysteriously by Benjamin Franklin and forwarded to the leaders of the Boston Sons of Liberty. The letters amounted to political blasting powder. Hutchinson had described his opponents in the colony as ignorant and irresponsible. Far worse, he had called for the suspension "of what are called English liberties . . . rather than the connexion [of Massachusetts] with the parent state should be broken."

Adams published the letters, and the public howled for Hutchinson's head. The assembly petitioned the North ministry for the governor's removal, without success. Government in Massachusetts became a shambles. Through the summer,

Hutchinson clung stubbornly to power, while the Sons of Liberty gained enough sympathizers and influence to block his every move.

The Boston Tea Party

The first tea ship sailed into tense Boston on November 27, 1773. Before the authorities could act to protect the *Dartmouth,* the Sons of Liberty had seized the ship and forced it to tie up under guard at Griffin's Wharf. A town meeting attended by five thousand people issued demands for the departure of the *Dartmouth* and the resignation of all tea consignees. Fearing mob violence, the consignees fled to Castle William in the harbor. Under pressure from Hutchinson, they refused to turn in their licenses.

The stalemate lasted nearly three weeks. Caught between the two sides was Francis Rotch, the young merchant who owned the *Dartmouth.* If he did not unload the ship's cargo, which included more than tea, by December 17, the government would seize it for nonpayment of duties. He requested permission to set sail for another port. Hutchinson refused but offered Rotch the protection of the Royal Navy. Rotch declined. He had seen the Sons of Liberty in action, and he very much wanted his ship, warehouse, home, and body left intact.

By December 16, the Sons of Liberty had also taken control of two more tea ships, the *Eleanor* and the *Beaver,* and tied them up near the *Dartmouth.* At a mass meeting that evening, an apologetic Rotch reported the governor's final refusal to let the *Dartmouth* sail. Adams dismissed the meeting by announcing that its members could do nothing more "to save their country." His words were a prearranged signal to a gang of the Sons of Liberty. About fifty men—dressed as Indians for no real

reason except the fun of it—rushed to Griffin's Wharf. In front of a cheering crowd, they boarded the ships, dragged the tea chests on deck, and dumped some ninety thousand pounds of tea into the harbor.

More than bitter tea brewed that night in Boston Harbor. In the litter of broken chests and the scum of tea leaves could be read a fearful message to the world: America stood on the brink of revolution.

The Sons of Liberty, dressed as Indians, throw cases of tea into Boston Harbor as a protest against the tea tax.

On the Eve of Revolution

Governor Hutchinson's report on the "tea party" arrived in London on January 27, 1774. The Privy Council, a largely ceremonial council of prominent men appointed by the king, met to discuss the outrage. The Council summoned Benjamin Franklin, the London agent for Georgia, New York, and Massachusetts. For two hours, one of the government's ministers heaped insults on America's most respected man.

Franklin took the abuse in silence. For years, he had worked for a fair arrangement that would give the colonies the freedom to grow *within* the British Empire. He left the council chamber with little hope for that future. He began preparing for the voyage home. Already nearly seventy, Franklin would soon become a passionate advocate of American independence.

The Intolerable Acts

After consulting the king, Prime Minister North began preparing a series of harsh measures to punish Massachusetts. Once the colonies saw the extent of Britain's anger, they would think twice before pulling the lion's whiskers again.

What Americans would call the Intolerable Acts were stern indeed. Until the dumped tea was paid for, the great port of Boston would be closed to all shipping except coastal vessels carrying food and fuel. The Massachusetts assembly would be deprived of much of its power, including the right to elect a council to advise the governor. Towns would no longer be allowed to call meetings except with the governor's permission. Most low-level officials would be appointed by the governor. His sheriffs would select juries to try defendants they themselves had arrested.

Some of the acts affected all the colonies. The Impartial Administration of Justice Act stated that a royal official accused of a major crime could be sent to another colony or to England for trial. A new quartering act stated that private families must take British soldiers into their homes when no other housing was available.

Although not intended as one of the Intolerable Acts, an additional law further enraged the northern colonists. The complicated Quebec Act expanded the boundaries of the Canadian province to include all the vast wilderness north of the Ohio River and east of the Mississippi. As far as the colonists were concerned, the Quebec Act was another attempt to frustrate their dreams of expansion westward.

To enforce the Intolerable Acts, the government dispatched General Thomas Gage and two regiments—three more were soon added—of infantry to Boston. Gage arrived on May 13, carrying his appointment as the new colonial governor. A discouraged Hutchinson handed over authority and made ready to leave his native Massachusetts forever. In the face of the overwhelming might of the occupying army, Adams and the Sons of Liberty went back to meeting in secret.

Support and Caution

The Intolerable Acts were denounced throughout the colonies. Colonial assemblies sent protests to London, and—to no one's great surprise—more than half of the assemblies were promptly suspended for exercising their right of free speech. Town meetings approved emergency shipments of food and other supplies for Boston. Heated debate raged on the risks and benefits of yet another boycott of British goods. There was even talk of gathering arms and gunpowder for a colonial army.

Amid the hubbub, some voices called for caution. In the population as a whole, the Sons of Liberty and their sympathizers amounted to only a fraction. Probably an equal number of people just as passionately—although less loudly—favored close ties with Britain. The Loyalists were willing to battle for colonial rights and the preservation of "the sacred rights of Englishmen," but not at the expense of angering an empire that—for all its faults—still gave its citizens more benefits and pride than nearly any on earth. For the Loyalists, Adams and his followers were loud, violent, and irresponsible "hotheads."

In 1774, a patriotic barber in New York, when half through shaving a British naval officer, learns his identity and refuses to finish the job.

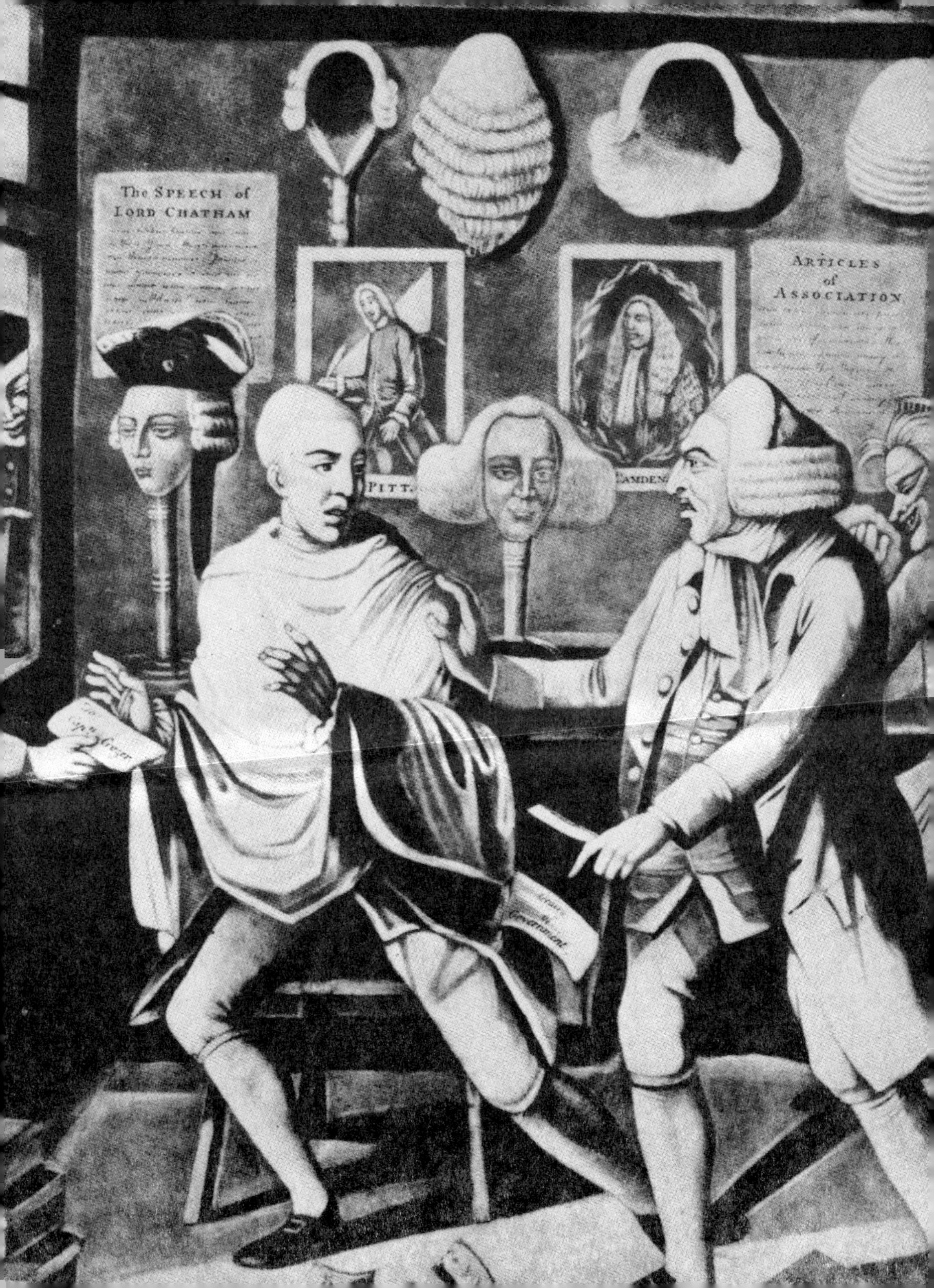
The SPEECH of
LORD CHATHAM
PITT
CAMDEN
ARTICLES
of
ASSOCIATION
Government

Probably a majority of the colonists felt caught between the two factions, wanting only the peace and quiet to go on about their lives. Yet nearly everyone, even those with little interest in politics, knew that some response must be sent to the government. Parliament's measures were truly intolerable. Massachusetts could not survive under them, nor could the other colonies continue doing business under the threat of similar treatment.

The First Continental Congress

In the tense summer of 1774, twelve of the colonies sent representatives to a congress in Philadelphia. Only Georgia, fearful that it might need regular British troops to put down an Indian uprising, decided against sending a delegation. The First Continental Congress brought together many of the most prominent and talented men in America. They represented a range of political views, but all shared the opinion that the situation was extremely serious.

When formal sessions began September 5, the Massachusetts delegation, which included Sam and John Adams, remained strangely quiet. The hothead label was much on their minds, and they decided to appear cool and moderate. The Virginia delegates took the lead in debate. They were a brilliant lot: George Washington, planter and soldier-hero of the French and Indian War; Patrick Henry, the famous orator; Richard Henry Lee, a debater at least equal to Henry; and the distinguished Peyton Randolph, speaker of the House of Burgesses and chairman of the Congress.

The Virginians argued hard for unified colonial action. Henry proclaimed, "The distinctions between Virginians, Pennsylvani-

George Washington en route to the First Continental Congress

Four Virginians shaped the direction of the First Continental Congress: (top) *George Washington and Patrick Henry;* (bottom) *Richard Henry Lee and Peyton Randolph.*

ans, New Yorkers, New Englanders are no more. I am not a Virginian, but an American!"

Such sentiments did not convince everyone. Many other southern delegates felt less kinship with the northerners. The northern colonies produced a variety of crops and a steadily increasing number of manufactured goods. They could survive without the mother country, but trade with Britain was the economic lifeblood of the southern colonies, which were dependent on one or two major crops. Even the Virginia delegation opposed any plan that would bar export of the next tobacco crop to Britain.

The Congress broke into committees in an attempt to resolve two critical questions: On what basis did colonial rights rest? What actions should the colonies take in response to the Intolerable Acts?

The committee on colonial rights wallowed for weeks in philosophical argument. A strong Loyalist faction led by Joseph Galloway of Pennsylvania championed Parliament's position. Yet, after much debate, the committee approved a statement that took the old "no taxation without representation" argument a step further by denying that Parliament had any rights whatsoever in the control of colonial affairs.

The committee discussing the response to the Intolerable Acts had even more difficulty. Behind the scenes, the Massachusetts delegation schemed furiously. They relayed news of the army's harsh methods in Boston. Paul Revere, Son of Liberty and untiring horseman, brought word that the people of Suffolk County, which included Boston, had resolved to form an independent government and arm themselves to resist the British army. In a fit of patriotic frenzy, the Congress endorsed the Suffolk Resolves.

Yet few in Congress were enthusiastic about the prospect of

war. Many delegates could imagine the benefits of independence, but few wished to face the unleashed might of Britain's army and navy. After long debate, Congress finally agreed to a set of economic measures. Several imports, including tea, were banned immediately. As of December 1, 1774, the colonies would stop importing all British products. In a compromise satisfactory to the southern colonies, a ban on the export of colonial products to Britain was delayed until September 10, 1775. Committees in all cities and towns would enforce the measures and denounce violators as "enemies of American liberty."

Deepening Crisis in Massachusetts

While the First Continental Congress debated, the crisis in Massachusetts was growing worse. The people refused to be ruled according to the Intolerable Acts. Local committees took charge of the government and the court system. Militia companies drilled in dozens of towns. Towns gathered arms and other supplies for new recruits. Minuteman companies were formed, their members pledging to answer a threat from British troops at a minute's notice.

The patriots' activity worried General Gage. Although he was the royal governor of the colony and commander in chief of

As war clouds threatened, minutemen companies formed in towns throughout the colonies, their members pledging to answer a threat from British troops at a minute's notice.

British forces in America, his real authority ended at the narrow strip of land connecting Boston with the mainland. On the other side of Boston Neck, the colony was in open revolt. What few Loyalists remained in Massachusetts had fled to Boston and the army's protection—or were keeping very quiet.

Gage had about 4,500 well-trained and well-armed troops in Boston, enough to win almost any possible battle with the ill-trained and ill-equipped militias. Yet he could not occupy an entire colony of some 250,000 people. He had to play for time, in the hope that the government in London and the Continental Congress could work out a political solution before a clash sparked open warfare.

The Powder Alarm

A strange incident called the Powder Alarm had already shown how little it might take to start a shooting war in Massachusetts. For many years, most county and town militias had stored their spare gunpowder and weapons in arsenals controlled by the colony's government. However, as tension had mounted during the summer of 1774, the militias had begun quietly withdrawing their supplies. Gage recognized the danger and moved to delay the arming of the militias.

On September 1, Gage dispatched 260 troops to the Quarry Hill powderhouse in Charlestown on the far side of Boston harbor. The handful of colonial militiamen guarding the powderhouse quickly abandoned their posts. The British seized what powder remained in the arsenal and returned to Boston without incident. However, rumors were soon spreading that an armed clash had left six militiamen dead.

The rumors spread with astonishing speed. In hours, thousands of angry militiamen and unorganized volunteers were

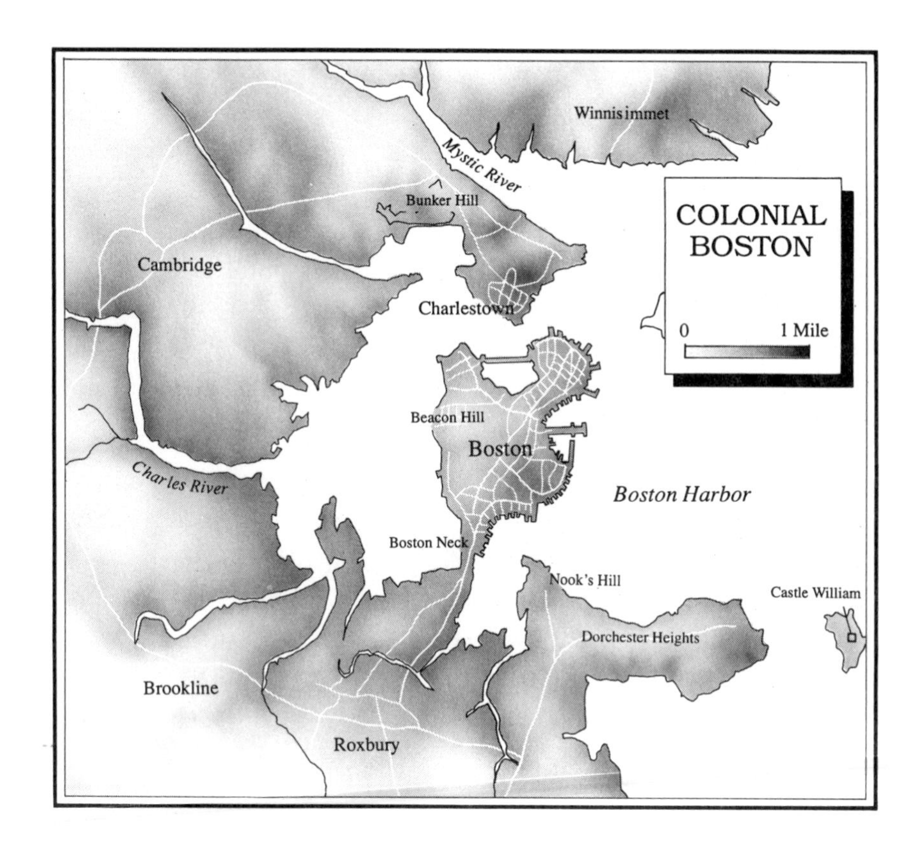

marching toward Boston. By the next day, four thousand men had assembled in Cambridge, less than three miles from the outskirts of Boston. An estimated twenty thousand more were coming from as far away as Connecticut. Some hotheads talked of besieging the British. So what if the rumor of a battle on Quarry Hill had been false? Gage was cornered in a hostile city almost surrounded by water. Why not evacuate the civilians and bombard the army into submission? Cooler heads prevailed. If there had to be war, the British must start it. Otherwise, Massachusetts might find itself alone in the fight. Everyone went home.

Gage Calls for Help

The Powder Alarm demonstrated that a large number of colonists were willing to fight on short notice. Gage ordered fortifications built across Boston Neck to protect the city from surprise attack. Townspeople sabotaged the work at every opportunity, but it continued until Boston lay virtually cut off from the mainland.

Meanwhile, Gage was busy writing reports to his superiors. He requested an additional twenty thousand troops. Until he had reinforcements—or a political solution could be found—he suggested that the Intolerable Acts be suspended to cool colonial anger.

Gage's opinions were not well received in London. Parliament and most of the government's ministers had been on vacation since late summer and little understood the depth of colonial anger over the Intolerable Acts. Furthermore, they did not believe Gage's warning that he no longer faced a mob of "Boston rabble," but the solid farmers and villagers of New England.

Prime Minister North informed the king of Gage's requests. The king rejected any thought of suspending the Intolerable Acts: "New England [being] in a state of rebellion, blows must decide whether they are to be subject to this country or independent."

Preparing for War

In New England, many people thought fighting could break out any day. The Massachusetts assembly, which now called itself the provincial congress, met in October 1774. It ignored Gage's angry demands that it dissolve and began making preparations for war. It voted a large sum for equipping a Massachusetts army and sent messages to the Rhode Island, Connecticut, and New Hampshire assemblies, suggesting the formation of a New England army of twenty thousand. To complete its preparations, the provincial congress empowered a five-man committee to order the militia into action. The powder keg now had a very short fuse, and Gage's messages to London took on an increasingly desperate tone.

Gage soon had more to report. In Massachusetts, the cannon standing in harbor batteries, or on village parks called greens, began disappearing in the night. Rhode Islanders carried off the entire forty-four-gun battery of Fort Island, near Providence. At Fort New Castle in New Hampshire, colonists overpowered the regular army guard, and seized several cannon, a tremendous amount of powder, and fifteen hundred muskets.

Petitioning the King

Amid the alarms and rumors of October 1774, the Continental Congress in Philadelphia was writing an appeal to King George. During the weeks of debate, the king had been openly criticized for the first time. In earlier crises, the colonists had heaped abuse on Parliament and the government, while still maintaining that they were loyal subjects of the king. But colonial patience was wearing thin; the king must take action to prevent a complete break between mother country and colonies. Congress decided not to send a similar petition to Parliament, further emphasizing its decision to deny Parliament any right to rule in America.

The First Continental Congress adjourned on October 26, 1774, resolving to meet again in the spring if circumstances required. The delegates hurried home. Many of them advised their colonies to make ready for war. In Fairfax County, Virginia, George Washington, the thirteen colonies' best known military leader, began whipping the local militia into shape. All but the most bloodthirsty hotheads in America still hoped that a peaceful solution could be found, but even such levelheaded men as John Adams feared otherwise.

Despite the dangers of further angering the mighty mother country, most Americans supported the economic measures voted by the Continental Congress. The boycott of British imports—still America's best weapon—went into effect December 1, 1774. By year's end, British imports had slowed to a trickle. Local committees enforced nonimportation ruthlessly. They seized goods, held up violators to public contempt, and, when all else failed, bashed a few heads. Passions were on the rise. Only an act of extraordinary statesmanship by the British government could prevent an explosion.

"If They Mean to Have War..."

Old, sick, but unfailingly courageous, William Pitt—the greatest British statesman of his generation—rose to address the House of Lords on January 20, 1775. He proposed a daring plan: Parliament should withdraw all British troops from America, recognize the Continental Congress as an official body, and repeal the Intolerable Acts. Pitt begged Parliament to listen to colonial complaints: "What is our right to persist in such cruel and vindictive measures against that loyal and respectable people?"

Pitt's great speech failed to win over the angry and stubborn members of the House of Lords. The majority supported the North government's policy of crushing colonial disobedience. For two weeks, Pitt and his allies in the House of Commons fought for fair treatment of the colonies, but all their proposals lost by wide margins.

Parliament set about passing yet another set of laws to punish the colonies. The new acts would pile more restrictions on colonial trade and completely close the rich waters off Canada to the New England fishing fleets. Prime Minister North sug-

gested a measure to attack colonial unity. Thinly disguised as a peace offering—an "olive branch" in North's words—Parliament would promise not to tax any colony that agreed to raise a yearly sum set by the government. The "olive branch" was an insult to colonial intelligence. A colonial assembly would have the dirty job of tax collecting but no say whatsoever in setting the total to be paid to the British government. Once again, the government was proposing taxation without representation.

Gage Prepares to Strike

In Boston, General Gage was a very worried man, as he waited for reinforcements and instructions from his government. One can imagine his frustration with the long delays. Gage was a professional soldier and a good one. He knew that the colonial militia was improving with every passing day. Many companies included veterans of the French and Indian War. By European standards, the militiamen might be rough, inexperienced, and undisciplined, but Massachusetts could raise a tremendous number of them. Gage would have to move soon or risk being bottled up in Boston.

Gage made plans to seize colonial munitions and the leaders of the provincial congress. He recruited informers and sent patrols to scout the countryside. If the government demanded

William Pitt, in a desperate attempt to prevent war, begged the British Parliament to listen to the colonists' complaints, but to no avail.

the use of force—and he suspected it would—a quick thrust might shatter colonial confidence. The danger lay in an actual fight with colonial troops. Would the nearly certain British victory discourage or enrage the colonists? The optimists on Gage's staff believed the former, but Gage warned his superiors again that the use of force could lead to war.

On April 14, 1775, Gage received a stinging letter from his government. The ministers could see no need for reinforcements to put down a "rude rabble" of colonists. Gage was to move as soon as possible to suppress the rebellion and arrest its leaders. If the use of force led to bloodshed, then better now than later.

Gage had his instructions and, despite doubts, he prepared to carry them out. He had already chosen his objectives. His informers had told him that the patriot leaders Samuel Adams and John Hancock were staying in Lexington, about nine miles from Boston. About seven miles farther west, the colonists had stored a large amount of supplies in Concord. A British force dispatched before dawn could make the thirty-two-mile round trip to Concord and be safely back in Boston by evening.

Watchful Eyes

The British could do little that was not soon known to the patriots. There were spies in England, and rebel leaders received a summary of the government's instructions to Gage almost a week before the actual letter arrived at the general's headquarters. In Boston, Dr. Joseph Warren's network of informers and spies soon detected Gage's preparations for the expedition.

By the evening of April 18, Warren knew the hour, size, and direction of the expedition. Before midnight, 350 light infantry and 350 elite grenadier guards, under the command of Colonel

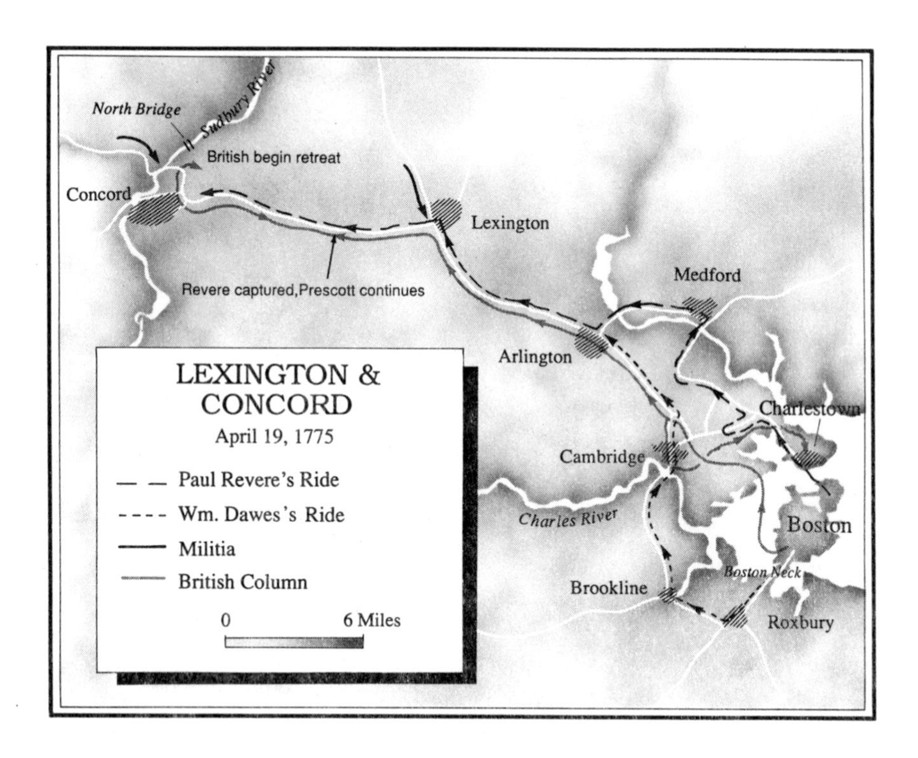

Francis Smith, would set off for Lexington and Concord. The repair of small boats in recent days indicated that the troops would probably cross the harbor to Charlestown and march northwest from there, rather than take the longer route over Boston Neck.

Warren's information was correct. The British troops were awakened about 10:00 P.M. and moved quietly through the streets to the harbor. Their march was supposed to be secret, but it was almost immediately detected. Warren dispatched two messengers to carry the news to Lexington and Concord. William Dawes slipped past the guard at Boston Neck. Paul Revere was rowed by two friends to Charlestown.

The Midnight Ride

Patriots in Charlestown had a horse waiting for Revere. He mounted and set out on his famous "midnight ride." After alerting villages and farms along his route, Revere arrived in Lexington about midnight. He awakened Adams and Hancock and told them to escape. Then, joined by Dawes and Dr. Samuel Prescott, Revere rode on toward Concord. A British patrol intercepted them. Prescott and Dawes escaped, but the soldiers took Revere's horse and left him to walk back to Lexington—a rather unromantic end to the "midnight ride of Paul Revere."

However, the messengers had done their job. By the time Prescott made it to Concord, the whole countryside was in turmoil as church bells and signal guns sounded the alarm. Militiamen pulled on their clothes, grabbed their muskets, and hurried off down the dark roads to join their units.

"The Shot Heard Round the World"

The British light infantry companies marched into Lexington at about 4:30 in the morning. Drawn up on the village green were about seventy militiamen under the command of Captain John Parker. The light infantry swung into battle formation facing the rebels. Confronted with the dismal prospect of backing down 350 of the king's best troops, some in Parker's formation suggested that it was madness to remain. Some historians would later credit Parker with the reply, "If they mean to have war, let it begin here."

It is doubtful that he actually spoke the famous words, and even if he did, he quickly reconsidered. The commander of the light infantry, Major John Pitcairn, and two or three of his officers rode forward and ordered the militia to "lay down your

The Lexington militia is fired upon by British troops under Major John Pitcairn— "the shot heard round the world."

arms . . . and disperse." Parker turned to his men and gave the order to break ranks, but said nothing about laying down their muskets. As the men started to hurry from the green carrying their weapons, Pitcairn shouted, "Damn you! Why don't you lay down your arms?" Another officer yelled, "Damn them. We will have them," apparently meaning the muskets.

The angry shouts of the officers may have been misinterpreted by one of the British soldiers as an order to fire. Or perhaps one of the militiamen fired by intent or by accident. No one ever determined who actually fired the single shot that touched off the American Revolution. The "shot heard round the world" was followed immediately by an order from a British officer to fire. A volley tore into the militia. A few colonial muskets answered. Pitcairn tried to stop the firing, but a second volley cut down more of the militia, including Captain Parker.

A cloud of powder smoke drifted away on the early morning breeze. Eight rebels lay dead or dying on Lexington Green, another ten carried wounds away, one British soldier had been creased by a bullet, and all hell was about to break loose.

On Concord Bridge

The grenadiers and Colonel Smith marched into Lexington cheering the victory of the light infantry. Any hope that the march could be kept secret had fled with the retreating militia. With fifes and drums playing, the British marched on to Concord. Along the way they could spot small groups of colonists running through the fields to get to the village ahead of them. What the redcoats could not see were the hundreds of militiamen hurrying toward Concord from towns thirty or more miles away.

The British column entered Concord about 7:00 A.M. The

local militia retreated over the bridge spanning the river west of town and took positions on Punkatasset Hill. Colonel Smith ordered about 175 light infantry to guard the bridge, dispatched 175 more to search houses on the far side, and set the grenadiers to searching the town.

The search found little. The rebels had already removed or safely hidden most of the munitions the British had come to capture. Either in anger or by accident, the grenadiers set fire to the blacksmith shop and the courthouse.

The militiamen—by this time numbering some four hundred strong—saw the smoke. A quick poll decided their course of action: they marched down the hill to defend the town or "die in the attempt." At the bridge, the light infantry fired on the militia, killing two and wounding one. The militia returned a heavier fire, killing three and wounding nine. The British fell back and the militia charged across the bridge, but then stopped to debate their next objective.

A few minutes later, the British troops sent to search the houses on the far side of the river dogtrotted over the bridge, past the silent muskets of the militia, and into town without a shot being fired.

The Retreat to Boston

Even the slow-witted Colonel Smith realized that his situation had become dangerous. Sixteen miles of hostile countryside lay between Concord and the safety of Boston. He re-formed his column and started the return march shortly after noon. For a mile, nothing happened; then a volley from the woods smashed into the column.

A strange, torturous battle had begun. On either side of the road, light infantry detachments tried to keep the rebels at a

The British troops retreat from Concord, fired on by colonists from the cover of trees, stone walls, houses, and barns.

distance. But news of the bloodshed on Lexington Green and Concord Bridge had enraged the colonists. They pressed in, fighting without central command and no plan other than to punish the redcoats. They fired on the column from the cover of trees, stone walls, houses, and barns. Some later historians would speak of excellent Yankee marksmanship. In reality, only about one of every three hundred bullets fired hit a British soldier. Yet by early afternoon, well over a thousand Americans had entered the battle, and their mass of fire was ferocious.

The once-proud British column was a disorderly mob of desperate men by the time it reached Lexington for the second time that day. Smith was wounded, and Pitcairn had lost his horse. Just when total destruction seemed certain, the soldiers heard a rattle of drums and caught a glimpse of crimson uniforms advancing from the southwest. A relief column of a thousand British soldiers marched into view.

A Long Agony

Brigadier General Earl Percy took command of the combined British force. He rested the troops for an hour before resuming the march to Boston at about 3:30 P.M. The troops looted and burned farmhouses on their way. At first the Americans seemed cowed by the large British force, but then they attacked with redoubled fury. There were now upwards of two thousand colonists shooting from the fields, woods, and houses. By the end of the afternoon, close to four thousand colonists would engage in the fighting.

The British fought back, striking hard at exposed parties of rebels. Houses were stormed and rebels bayonetted before they could surrender. At villages and farms, redcoats and rebels fought hand to hand, bayonets against musket butts and axes. Percy's men pushed their way through stiff resistance in Menotomy (today's Arlington). In Cambridge, the fighting was house to house for a mile and a half.

The afternoon was far advanced by the time Percy's troops made it through Cambridge. The final miles to Boston Neck promised more heavy fighting, and darkness would aid the rebels. Percy swung his column to the east and marched toward Charlestown.

Shortly after sunset, the long agony ended as the exhausted British troops reached the safety of the harbor and the protection of the Royal Navy's guns. A count of the casualties found that British losses were 73 killed, 174 wounded, and 26 missing. The colonists would later calculate their losses at 49 killed, 41 wounded, and 5 missing.

By most standards, it had been a small battle. The forces engaged were not large, the casualties surprisingly light for the number of bullets fired. But history records few battles with more important consequences.

☆ 7 ☆

Revolution

A crescent of campfires stretched from Boston Neck to Charlestown on the chilly evening of April 18, 1775. For the colonists staring across the harbor to the flickering lights of Boston, the night must have been alive with a hundred emotions. The tensions of a decade of dispute had let loose in a day of savage battle. They had fired on the soldiers of the king, the infantry of the most feared army on earth. What would come of those long hours of killing? Few believed that the bloodshed had ended with the sunset or doubted that the sun would rise on a future filled with danger.

Not a few must have regretted that revolution had come to America. There had been the horror of seeing both friends and foes fall wounded or dead. Some men wrestled with the terrible knowledge that they had killed fellow human beings. And there was fear. The British Empire was huge, its power immense. The mighty Royal Navy could strangle colonial trade and land vast armies of redcoated soldiers anywhere on the long coastline of the thirteen colonies. Who was to say that even the threat of an attack might not tear apart the fragile unity of the colonies? Might the Revolution turn quickly into a civil war, colony against colony, neighbor against neighbor?

Yet along with the regret and the fear, the fatigue and the horror, there was also a sense of beginning. The future now lay in colonial hands, not those of a distant king and Parliament. Few of the men shivering by the campfires could guess what lay ahead on the long, hard road to independence, but they knew the journey had begun.

Suggested Reading

Ketchum, Richard, ed. *The Revolution.* New York: American Heritage, 1958.

McDowell, Bart. *The Revolutionary War.* Washington: National Geographic Society, 1967.

Middlekauff, Robert. *The Glorious Cause.* New York: Oxford University Press, 1982.

Poindexter, Jean. *Lexington and Concord, 1775: What Really Happened.* New York: Hastings House, 1975.

Smith, Robert. *The Infamous Boston Massacre.* New York: Crowell-Collier, 1969.

Ward, Christopher. *The War of the Revolution.* New York: Macmillan, 1952.

Wright, Esmond. *The Fire of Liberty.* New York: St. Martin's, 1983.

Index

About the Author

Alden R. Carter is a versatile writer for children and young adults. He has written nonfiction books on electronics, supercomputers, radio, Illinois, and the People's Republic of China. His novels *Growing Season* (1984) and *Wart, Son of Toad* (1985) were named to the American Library Association's annual list of best books for young adults. His most recent novel is *Sheila's Dying*. His other books on the American Revolution are: *Darkest Hours, At the Forge of Liberty,* and *Birth of the Republic.* Mr. Carter lives with his wife, Carol, and their son, Brian Patrick, and daughter, Siri Morgan, in Marshfield, Wisconsin.